Intellectual Property for Paralegals:
The Law of Trademarks, Copyrights, Patents, and Trade Secrets

(Second Edition)

Theory and also from Status Characteristic Theory (E.G. Cohen, forthcoming).

The conclusion to be drawn from this discussion is that a CRP is *inclusive* not exclusive, although for growth to be possible and recognizable, a CRP must have boundaries even if they are fuzzy. A program is not restricted to a single school of thought nor to the disciples of a particular sociologist. Programs entail a division of labor, so that critics of an idea or approach play as significant a role as champions of the idea; research intended to disconfirm an explanation stands equal to research intended to support the idea. CRPs are inclusive in two other respects: (1) CRPs require both theoretical and empirical activities and (2) CRPs involve empirical research employing the whole range of available research techniques—qualitative and quantitative, observational and experimental, primary analysis of documents and secondary analysis of existing data sets. We emphasize this because we believe that some sociological "schools" have fostered an exclusiveness of method—only qualitative analysis or only surveys or only experiments—that is detrimental to their own purposes and to the development of knowledge in general. To be sure, not every approach is suitable at every stage of development, but nothing is excluded *a priori*; choices depend on the nature of the question and the available knowledge base.

GENERAL QUESTIONS FOR A CRP

CRPs begin and grow in many ways, not all of which result from deliberate planning or conscious intent. Scientists, however, strive to make science as rational as possible; attempts to plan and direct the development of a CRP through careful analysis and with an explicit strategy serve to enhance the rational elements of the enterprise. To this end, we propose some aids to the analysis and planning of CRPs.

Some general questions apply to every stage of development of a CRP; others have more limited applicability and fit only early or only more advanced stages. In many respects these questions overlap with questions one would ask when focusing on a single study, but even when the questions are similar, asking them in the context of a CRP has quite different consequences. First, we will consider some questions one can pose at any stage and then we will examine early, intermediate, and advanced stages and the issues tied to each.

Two central questions guide researchers oriented to a CRP: (1) How can a proposed study build on previous knowledge and (2) How can future investigators build on the proposed study regardless of its outcome? Anyone who has ever been trained in research has learned to ask these questions; the mandatory review of the literature addresses the first question and the more optional "suggestions for future research" often deals with the second. Unfortunately, both literature reviews and discussions of future research have taken on a highly ritualistic character. Literature reviews tend to be unsystematic, uncritical, and undiscriminating, citing anyone the reviewer has uncovered who has worked in the general area[6] or used the same terms, whether or not the terms signified similar ideas. Many reviewers do not use the ideas or findings of cited works in any serious way and, in the extreme case, the review represents little more than scientific name-dropping. Part of the problem arises from the nature of publication in scientific journals; severe space limitations force writers to present unannotated lists of citations without discussion or analysis.[7] Similarly, sociologists too often treat suggestions for future research as afterthoughts, formulated post hoc to justify the importance of the study.

Both issues, how the study will build on prior knowledge and how future investigations will build on the study, require in-depth examination *before* conducting the research. At the very least, a researcher should formulate the immediate next step for each likely outcome of the study. The exercise of delineating likely outcomes for a study can be highly informative and constructing next steps can offer a sound basis for evaluating the significance of the proposed research. Particular next steps depend on the stage of development of the program, but raising the question is in order at every stage.

Determining how a study will build on prior knowledge necessitates an assessment of the knowledge base. When the knowledge base contains one or more theories, the theory or theories structure the assessment. While we cannot simply count the number of supporting studies relative to the number of disconfirming studies, we can examine the circumstances where the theory succeeds in explaining empirical findings and the circumstances where it fails. We can also consider the set of alternative explanations against which the theory has been tested. Such analyses should suggest problematic areas that need further empirical study. Alternatively, where problematic areas may not be of interest to a sociologist, he or she may undertake generalizing the theory or applying it to a practical problem.

Where the knowledge base does not contain an explicit theory, assessment poses many more difficulties. We are only beginning to appreciate the shortcomings of most assessments and the inherent obstacles to determining what we know (Light and Pillemer, 1984). In the absence of theory or at least some well-defined concepts, how do we deal with the fact that studies occur in different

---

6. Area boundaries are taken very broadly and inclusively. This is perhaps a hangover from the student researcher's concern with demonstrating familiarity with everything on the professor's reading list and showing the appropriate erudition. The norm seems to be ''Cite everything you read whether or not you make any use of it.'' While that may be an appropriate part of scholarly rites of passage, it sometimes inhibits rather than fosters the growth of knowledge.

7. Of course, published articles may not reflect the extensive thinking that went into the research but, if that is the case, it defeats the purpose of publishing, that is, communicating ideas to other researchers. We should also note that where well-developed theoretical traditions exist, such citation lists inform initiated readers quite well; each tradition provides a common culture so that citing name and date triggers an appropriate set of associations in the reader's mind. When such lists occur in the absence of a well-defined tradition or research program, they exemplify ritualistic exercises even when the author has the best of intentions; the average reader will be both unfamiliar with the majority of the works cited and not usually interested enough to look them up and read them. In such cases, citations communicate little to the reader beyond the fact that the researcher did some reading.

settings, institute varying controls on the situation and/or the data gathering procedure, collect different observations, summarize them in different ways, provide diverse interpretations, use dissimilar modes of inference, and so on? Some assessments read like laundry lists, presenting finding after finding from studies that presumably all deal with the topic of the review. Without conceptualization, however, deciding that the studies in fact deal with the same topic is itself problematic, as we commented earlier.

The notion that we can list the totality of findings and determine an "average" result rests on an additive conception of cumulation that implicitly defines knowledge as the sum of empirical findings. The approach has several inadequacies: (1) it tacitly assumes the generalizability of observation statements; (2) it begs the question of comparability; (3) it assigns equal weights to every study, ignoring differences in importance or quality of work; and (4) it does not discriminate among types of variables such as variables reflecting artifacts, controls, scope restrictions, and substantive explanations. Operating on these assumptions leads to assessments that exaggerate the disarray in the field, discourage researchers, and suggest to consumers that sociologists do not know what they are doing. Most assessments do not fit this "worst case" scenario, but few avoid all of the pitfalls.

Developing criteria for the assessment of the state of knowledge challenges those interested in the methodology of CRPs. While we cannot offer specific suggestions, we believe that our conception of cumulation points to an approach. Viewing cumulation as an increase in the capacity to define and solve theoretical or practical problems leads naturally to a set of questions. What problems does the research area define? How have these problem-definitions changed over time? What aspects of what phenomena do researchers attempt to explain? What alternative explanations have they considered? Which of these alternatives have they rejected? Have the researchers attempted to generalize their explanations? How has the research area dealt with artifacts and observation error? What improvements in research techniques have occurred over time?

For applied and engineering programs, we can ask the same questions and add a few more. What do investigators regard as the critical features of the treatment or intervention? Do the treatments examined in evaluation studies have all of these critical features? Does variation in the degree to which critical features are present help to explain variations in treatment evaluation? Do treatment evaluations deal with uniform outcomes? If not, to what extent are outcomes comparable and does the heterogeneity of outcomes studied help to explain differences in treatment evaluation? What alternative explanations for treatment success or failure have been considered? Have researchers attempted to formulate sets of conditions under which the intervention leads to desired outcomes? To be sure, many practitioners and policy makers ask some of these questions, but we cannot take for granted that every treatment evaluation takes a similar or equally systematic approach.

Assessment that is both intersubjective and systematic requires more than asking a set of questions; we need criteria for evaluating the answers. The proposed questions, however, provide a starting point because they exemplify a different orientation to assessment. We believe that using questions such as these can contribute to systematizing the reviews of past work as well as to more rational planning of future work. At the very least, this orientation should avoid the difficulties inherent in attempting to add up the apples and oranges of diverse studies.

A basic assumption underlying the argument for CRPs is that research strategy depends on the nature of the problem. Certainly what we already know and understand constitutes one important aspect of the nature of the problem. The kinds of problems that we can identify and solve at any given time play a key role in deciding next steps and in evaluating the outcomes of those next steps. In short, both strategic choices and criteria for evaluation depend to a significant extent on the stage of development of a CRP. The next chapter will describe and examine early, intermediate, and more advanced stages of CRP in order to illustrate how criteria vary with developmental stage.

SUGGESTED READINGS

Lakatos, Imre, and Alan Musgrave, eds. *Criticism and the Growth of Knowledge.* Cambridge: Cambridge University Press, 1970.

This collection of essays deals with many of the issues raised here. Some understanding of the positions of Popper and Kuhn are necessary for a full appreciation of the discussion in these papers.

SIXTEEN

Stages
of a CRP

We noted that stages of a CRP are reconstructions based on the wisdom of hindsight. Even with this wisdom, boundaries between stages are, at best, fuzzy. We cannot claim today that a particular CRP has developed as far as, say, the fifth stage and we probably never will be able to make that kind of statement. However, as long as we don't demand too fine discrimination, we can make some distinctions without the benefit of hindsight. Although some disagreement might occur, researchers by and large can agree that a program is in a relatively early stage or a relatively well-developed stage and also, perhaps, that a program is closer to one or the other. For our purposes, we don't require fine distinctions and so we will group developmental stages into three categories: early, intermediate, and more advanced.

Sociologists have conducted studies on a vast array of different topics, but many of these studies have not generated subsequent research, and so they did not begin research programs. In some problem areas, programs have begun but have remained for a long period of time in relatively early stages of development. Various reasons account for the lack of follow-up of a study, or the lack of growth in a CRP; among them are intractability of the subject matter, flaws in the design or execution of the study or studies, or loss of interest in the topic. But intractability of subject matter, poor quality of initial work and low interest cannot account for all the cases where a program was stillborn or remained stagnated in an early stage. Some of this failure to advance results from an inadequate appreciation of how knowledge grows. Explicating properties of stages of a CRP cannot make intractable problems disappear, but it can provide stimulus to growth by increasing our understanding of the growth process.

In this chapter, we will describe and analyze early, intermediate, and more advanced stages of a CRP. We will use the model for research developed in this book as our analytic tool because we believe that using our model provides direction for assisting the growth of a program. The three main sections of this chapter will spell out the properties of each stage and the requirements for further advancing a program. Our objective is to encourage producers of sociological knowledge to think in new ways about the research enterprise and to provide consumers with additional criteria for evaluating research claims.

EARLY STAGES OF A CRP

Every CRP begins with exploratory activities, either conceptual or empirical. As we noted in chapter 13, *exploratory studies* represent early attempts to gain knowledge about phenomenon or a situation; these have little foundation of theory, prior knowledge claims, or prior observations on which to build and often use observations to sharpen vaguely formulated ideas. Sociologists have conducted good exploratory studies in virtually every area of the field, but, in too many instances, we have not added to the knowledge gained in these initial ventures. Hence, one of the main problems is how to advance beyond the initial exploratory study.

Sociological knowledge deals with statements about sociological phenomena. In the earliest stages, we attempt to identify a phenomenon and to make some initial statements about aspects of the phenomenon that are of sociological interest. Early research on small group interaction observed differential participation among group members and differential ratings by group members of one another. The investigators believed that if such differences were stable and varied in a systematic way, these aspects of group behavior would be sociologically interesting. Part of this "interest" was the belief that sociological ideas could explain these features of group behavior. In the early stages, we ask: What is the phenomenon? What aspects are of interest? How stable are these aspects? In other words, what do we want to explain and is it stable enough so that we can explain it?

Some exploration starts with an idea and looks for phenomena that exemplify the idea. Durkheim started with the idea of a collective conscience and sought manifestations of it in various apects of social life. Typically, in the initial stage of a program, the sociologist has a new way of looking at phenomena and tries to determine how fruitful the new way is. Does the idea relate phenomena that were previously unrelated? Does the idea explain things that were inexplicable? Or does it explain them in a way that generates previously unrecognized consequences? In the early stages, vague formulations predominate and researchers, particularly the inventors of the idea, usually overestimate the idea's fruitfulness.

An attempt to solve a practical problem sometimes initiates CRP. During World War II, a government agency tried to convince groups of housewives to switch from scarce meats like steaks to more readily available variety meats like hearts and lungs; attempts to accomplish this generated a series of studies on interpersonal influence and group decision making. Many spin-offs from army research generated by concerns for military morale, reported in *The American Soldier* (Stouffer et al., 1949), contributed to programs in a number of areas of sociology. Despite these notable examples, many studies undertaken for engineering purposes remain "one-shot" affairs.

In terms of our model, one important set of activities in the early stages of a CRP involves turning vague, loosely formulated ideas into more precisely stated knowledge claims. A starting point might be an explanation based on singular premises and the next step could involve generating universal statements from the argument. Or the investigator might begin with an implicit hunch that must be formulated before it can be communicated to others. In the Expectation States Program, the intuitive notion that participation in a group could be explained by people's views about one another's ability became the knowledge claim: *Self-other expectations determine the observed power and prestige order.*

Lateral accumulation of observation statements makes up a substantial portion of the empirical research in the early stages of a program, in part to demonstrate the stability of the phenomenon and in part to justify concern with it. The body of research documenting social class effects on variables ranging from mortality to voting behavior in part served these purposes.

In the early stages, concepts are rarely defined explicitly and indicators are not well developed; the initial conditions linking ideas to observations are assumed to be true rather than tested and observations are taken because they are accessible rather than because they are optimally relevant to ideas. Needless to say, formal deductive argument plays almost no role in the initial stages of a program.

The goal of demonstrating that an idea has some explanatory power can focus much of the activity in the early stages of program. Without an indication of an idea's power, the relevant public has little reason to pay attention to it. Novel ideas that fail to explain any observation statements are about as newsworthy as the headline, "Dog bites man," and journals are about as likely to publish untested new ideas as a newspaper is to carry such a headline. And since, in most cases, communication to the relevant public requires journal publication, journal referees must be convinced that an idea has significant consequences. Both theoretical argument and empirical data can provide this demonstration.

Before any new empirical studies were undertaken, Expectation States researchers argued on theoretical grounds for the explanatory power of their first important knowledge claim[1] relating status characteristics to observed power and prestige orders in task-oriented groups. They claimed that this proposition could explain many sets of empirical findings ranging from the effects of race and gender to the consequences of military rank. After the theoretical paper was published, the first empirical studies in this program provided further indications of explanatory power. Creating artificial differences between actors on contrived status characteristics, the researchers produced corresponding differences in who influenced whom. These experiments allowed researchers to eliminate some alternative explanations including those based on chance and those based on differential familiarity with the group task.

In the early stages of development, disconfirmation is not very informative because the prime objective is to show explanatory power; as we have indicated,

---

1. See chapter 11.

new ideas are more likely to fail than to succeed. Furthermore, the nature of the alternative explanations is not a major concern and ideas are often tested against quite weak alternatives including explanations that an empirical result was due to chance. Most investigators believe that if weak alternatives like chance cannot be rejected in favor of the researcher's idea, then the idea does not have enough power to be worth pursuing. Given that the chance explanation prevails in reproducible tests, the belief has considerable merit. What must be emphasized is that rejection of chance as an explanation is only the beginning, not the end, of the process. Once we have shown that our ideas have some explanatory power, however, and are able to reproduce the success, we are ready for the intermediate stages.

INTERMEDIATE STAGES

When the researchers have demonstrated the stability of the phenomena of concern and have formulated one or more Simple Knowledge Structures which explain their observation statements, the program has advanced to a new level of development. Although there may be several advances in the early stages, and no sharp demarcation between early and intermediate stages of development is possible, we view early stages as complete when the proponents accept the program as viable and begin to spread out from their starting points. A stable phenomenon and some successful demonstrations of explanatory power represent minimal conditions of viability.

Spreading out can take a number of directions. Researchers can refine the ideas and techniques they use; they can explicate their concepts; they can generalize the knowledge claims; they can confront stronger alternative explanations; they can look for practical applications of their explanatory principles.

Sociologists working in the status characteristics program undertook refinement, generalization, and practical application. From the early focus on initiation of interaction, the idea of an *observable power and prestige order* led to other indicators including such things as *giving action opportunities, influence attempts, and resistance to other's influence attempts.* These concepts provided the basis for a standardized experimental situation which used the probability of a self-response given a disagreement with one's partner as the principal indicator. The notion of status characteristic became an explicitly defined concept, Diffuse Status Characteristics,[2] and later on the parallel concept of Specific Status Characteristic was added. Expanding the set of initial conditions and refining the concept of status characteristics not only suggested new empirical studies, but brought to bear a whole body of prior research on social influence that was previously unrelated to the idea that status beliefs affect interaction. Looking at previous research in this new light generated new questions that stimulated the formation of status characteristic theory.

---

2. See chapter 11.

A number of different activities can contribute to the refinement of the ideas of a CRP. We can investigate alternative initial conditions, thereby generating new hypotheses and new situations in which to test them against observation statements. Often, adding initial conditions will represent attempts to eliminate additional artifactual explanations; or it may involve testing a knowledge claim against stronger substantive alternatives than those based on the operation of chance factors. Some of these activities could lead to new ways to observe and measure our concepts and could dovetail with efforts to develop explicit definitional systems which, in turn, could stimulate further refinement of indicators. As new indicators are proposed, researchers may undertake reliability and validity studies.

When we have formulated a knowledge claim and scope conditions, we can begin to expand the explanatory power of our ideas. As we have delineated the process, generalizing takes place in two ways: (1) We can modify the scope restrictions and attempt to apply our knowledge claim to new situations and (2) we can construct an explanation of the knowledge claim itself in terms of more general premises and, in so doing, we can begin to formulate a theory. In the status characteristics program, constructing an explanation of the phenomenon preceded modifications of scope restrictions. The explanation was the first formulation of the theory.

The attempt to explain the knowledge claim that beliefs about status affect the way people interact raises questions of how and why this happened. Once the questions are asked, it is not difficult to generate answers; but many of the answers would not increase our knowledge because they would not be testable. The problem here is not simply to explain the knowledge claim, but to put the explanation in a form that would be testable and would advance the understanding of the phenomenon. We require an explanation that allows us to derive new consequences beyond our original explanandum, new consequences which generate new empirical tests. If these new tests confirm our new hypotheses, we have increased the power of our explanation.

The inventors of status characteristic theory wanted to answer the *how* and *why* questions in a way that would generate new testable consequences. They reasoned that, in performing tasks, people wanted to be successful and, in order to be successful, they needed to estimate their own and other people's ability at the task. If a person knew about the relative competence among group members, it was reasonable to expect that person to defer to those who were more competent and to expect deference from those who were less competent; furthermore, it was reasonable to assume that a person would accept influence from those who were more competent and resist influence from those who were less competent. In the absence of direct information about relative competence at the task, perhaps status information or beliefs about status provided cues to task competence. The reader will recall from chapter 11 that these ideas were incorporated in the concepts of *general expectation state* and *gamma* (γ) *set*. The theorists then formulated a set of assumptions that linked these ideas to performances in specific task situations. The assumptions answered the *why* question: because beliefs about status provide

needed cues about task abilities. The theory answered the *how* question by describing a process by which these beliefs become relevant to a task. As we saw in chapters 11 and 12, the explanation led to several additional derivations and to new testable hypotheses. The first study testing the theory had three treatments, each of which tested a different derivation and each of which provided evidence consistent with the derived knowledge claim.

At one point, the program confronted a disconfirmation. Dealing with this disconfirmation contributed to the growth of the theory, even though the proposed solution was later rejected. Seashore (1968) compared a treatment which had white students interacting on a task with a person they were told was black with another treatment in which a similar group of white students interacted with a person they were told was white. The researcher assumed that for white students in the United States in the 1960s, race was a status characteristic and assumed that the state *white* was higher than the state *black.* The comparison treatment created a situation in which the students believed that their partner was of a higher status. (The reason for this choice of comparison treatment will be discussed later.) According to the theory, students who believed their partners were black should have been more resistant to influence than students who believed their partners were higher status whites, but the study found no difference between the two treatments.

The failure of this study to support its hypothesis confronted the researchers with a difficult choice. The theory could be false, or the initial condition that race was an instance of a status characteristic could be false, or some other factor could explain the failure. Because the theory had already received several confirmations, the theorists were reluctant to abandon it. The historical situation of the United States in the 1960s might have negated the initial condition of race as an instance of a status characteristic; after all, one goal of the civil rights movement was to change expectations that blacks are less competent than whites. Despite some success of the movement, it seemed premature to regard the initial condition as false. Researchers turned to the third option and sought some other factor to explain the disconfirmation.

In an effort to explain the failure of the study to support the theory, Cohen et al. (1969) examined the study design in close detail. They found that when participants were told that their partner was black, they were given additional information. They were informed, for example, that their partner was the same age as themselves, in order to make it less obvious that race was the subject of the study. From the point of view of the theory, this design feature was perfectly reasonable. But *age* also could be a diffuse status characteristic, and the researchers were forced to consider the possibility that the consequences of being equals on one status characteristic might override the consequences of being differentiated on another. Close reading of chapter 11 reveals that the theory takes no stand on the issue of status equality except in scope condition 5. Scope condition 5 asserts that the actors cannot be equals on all status characteristics and it requires that the status characteristic in question be the only social basis of discrimination between actors. The theory applies, then, when the actors are differentiated on one diffuse status characteristic and are equals on other potentially operating characteristics. The disconfirming study was therefore, clearly within the scope of the theory. Yet the possible explanation that being equal in age outweighed being different in race deserved to be investigated.

A new study was designed which essentially repeated the two treatments of the original investigation, but added two new treatments. The new treatments omitted any information that participants might construe as indicating that they and their partners were status equals; thus, they were not told that they and their partner were the same age. The four treatments and their significant features were as follows:

Treatment *A*: Participant told that partner was higher status white; no other status information given.

Treatment *B*: Participant told that partner was higher status white who was same age as participant.

Treatment *C*: Participant told that partner was black who was same age as participant.

Treatment *D*: Participant told that partner was black; no other status information given.

Treatments *B* and *C* were the treatments of the original study; and, again, no differences in resistance to influence were found between these two treatments. The repeat study supported the reliability of the findings of the original investigation and eliminated the uniqueness explanation. But differences consistent with the theory were found between treatments *A* and *D*; participants in treatment *D* were more resistant to influence than participants in treatment *A*. This result supported the speculation that the consequences of status equality accounted for the failure of the original study to support the theory.

Cohen et al. (1969) proposed a modification of scope condition 5 to rule out other bases for forming expectations such as other status characteristics where p' and o possessed the same or equivalent states. The modified scope was consistent with the intent of the original theory to deal exclusively with situations where there was only a single discriminating characteristic, and it meant that Seashore's study need not be considered a disconfirmation. Later, however, Berger et al. (1977) generalized the theory to multicharacteristic situations, and scope condition 5 was no longer needed. The 1977 generalization greatly increased the theory's explanatory power and represented a new developmental stage of the program.

The use of "equating characteristics," status characteristics where p' and o possessed the same or equivalent states, to explain the Seashore result seemed fruitful at the time. Several later studies (e.g., Webster, 1977, and Martin and Sell, 1985) have indicated that actors ignore information from equating characteristics; this contrasts with the results of Seashore (1968) and Cohen et al. (1969). While these more recent experiments differ in some respects from the 1968 and 1969 studies—for example, in how directly relevant the differentiating characteristics were to the task—they do argue against the explanation put forward by Cohen et al. Now that much more is known about the operation of equating character-istics, it seems that we need to look elsewhere for an explanation of the Seashore experiment and the Cohen et al. replication. Nevertheless, these two experiments played a role in the development of the theory even if their original explanation has been discarded; growth, after all, is not a simple linear process.

As a CRP grows, applied research using the program's knowledge becomes possible. Sometimes the ideas of the program provide new ways of looking at famil-iar problems as, for example, when organizational studies document the conse-quences of informal leadership (Dalton, 1959) or when sex role investigations point to the results of gender differentiation in the world of work (Treiman and Terrell, 1975). Sometimes the tools of a program play a role in forecasting social trends; when social mobility researchers developed techniques for measuring occupational mobility, some applied researchers used these to forecast a society's future occup-tional structures. One of the most sophisticated types of application occurs when a theory is used to design interventions for the solution of a practical problem. In the status characteristic program, once the theory had been formulated, sociol-ogists concerned with problems of minority group children in the classroom devel-oped interventions to increase both the participation and academic achievement of these children (Entwisle and Webster, 1974; E. G. Cohen and Roper, 1972).

We can sum up the features of intermediate stages of the process. Concerns include: (1) expanding the explanatory power of a simple knowledge structure through formulation of a theory and/or modifying the scope condition, (2) refin-ing concepts and observational techniques using explicit definitions and reliability-validity studies, and (3) testing the applicability of the program to other research areas and/or practical problems. There is an interdependence of the theoretical and empirical investigation. The derivation of new hypotheses occurs through the substitution of alternative sets of initial conditions—the explicit definition of con-cepts and the generalization of the knowledge claim. Generalizing the knowledge claim involves both formulating assumptions from which it can be deduced and modifying the set of scope conditions. On the empirical side, the explanations of the program confront alternative explanations, some of which may be only slight modifications of the original ideas. During intermediate stages of a CRP, both confirmation and disconfirmation of the derived hypotheses are informative; both instances where substantive explanations prevail over alternatives and instances where they do not can generate advances in the program, as the example of scope conditions illustrated. Of course, whether or not the program moves forward depends on the nature of the alternative explanations—ad hoc alternatives rarely contribute to growth—and the quality of analysis of both success and failure.

MORE ADVANCED STAGES

To say that we are at an advanced stage of the process requires that we have one or more explicitly formulated theories and a substantial number of empirical confirmations. This does not mean that all empirical research supports the theory or theories; theories can and do persist despite some disconfirming studies. We think of CRPs in more advanced stages as mature programs in which theories have considerable explanatory power and where the program has a clear record of generating and solving problems. But theories are not final truths; hence there is no end to the process. As with all scientific knowledge, the theories of a CRP are provisional and can always be improved.

Unless the program continues to generate new research, defining and solving new theoretical and/or practical problems, the program will die. Development of knowledge cannot rest on past accomplishments, but must continue to show potential for new understanding, or scientists will lose interest. Engineering tools may be a legacy of a CRP but engineering achievements alone will not sustain a CRP; development of knowledge will move to a new arena. In a sense, twentieth century classical physics illustrates the phenomenon; whatever research occurs in classical physics tends to be done by engineers as physicists have moved into other problem areas like high energy or solid state physics.

In sociology, we do not have any CRPs comparable to classical physics with its record of successes spread over three centuries. Nevertheless, the same processes operate in, and the same concerns apply to, the development of sociological knowledge. While some sociological CRPs have passed through the intermediate stages, many have died out before reaching more advanced stages even though they may have demonstrated some success. In part, excessive effort invested in lateral accumulation may account for the loss of sociological interest in some programs. While there are no road maps to scientific breakthroughs, a more developed methodology of CRPs could prove guidance for researchers working in mature programs. The discussion that follows may lay a foundation for guiding the development and evaluation of CRPs in more advanced stages of development.

More advanced stages of development have two characteristic features: programs branch out and programs compete with one another (Wagner and Berger, 1985). Branching occurs when scientists develop parallel theories employing the same concepts and core ideas to explain different domains of phenomena as, for example, when Emerson's theory of power-dependence relations in interpersonal behavior (Emerson, 1962) becomes the basis of a theory of interorganizational phenomena (Pfeffer and Salancik, 1978). Programs compete by direct confrontations of alternative theories as explanations for a given set of phenomena. Demonstration that one CRP has greater explanatory power than another requires both logical and empirical tests.

Very few sociological programs are at an advanced stage of development where a choice among alternatives is the focus of attention. Of course, there is a "confrontation" between functional sociologists and conflict sociologists: the former argue that societies are fundamentally stable because they fulfill basic human needs; the latter assert that societies are fundamentally unstable because the needs of one group are incompatible with the needs of others. Neither of these programs would meet the requirements for an advanced stage of a CRP. The formulations of both the conflict and the structural-functional perspectives are not sufficiently explicit to allow intersubjective agreement on what constitutes a disconfirmation of their knowledge claims.

Disconfirmation, where the hypothesis deduced from the theory is inconsistent with an observation statement or particularly where the theory's explanation is rejected in favor of one from an alternative CRP, is an important criterion at this stage. If a theory has received a number of confirmations, one more confirmation, even if reproducible, does not add much weight. Reproducible disconfirmation, however, can be very informative—indicating problems the theorists have not solved or, at least, indicating the limits of a theory's explanatory power. A direct challenge occurs if a theory from a particular CRP fails while an alternative theory from a competing CRP succeeds. If there are only a few such occurrences, the impact on the first program will be relatively minimal. Of course, each clear confrontation motivates researchers to look for other ways to pit one program against the other. If neither CRP dominates the other in these confrontations, then the programs can coexist as long as each generates and solves new problems. The theories in each program may undergo modification or it may become clear that the programs succeed in different domains. Alternatively, the programs may differentiate so that one deals, for example, with an *intra*organizational domain while the other focuses on *inter*organizational phenomena. If one CRP regularly succeeds where the other fails, we may have the beginning of the end for the failing program unless, of course, the program simultaneously has some striking successes. Scientific integrity, however, requires each of us to be willing to give up a program under some set of circumstances. While researchers may vary in their thresholds for stagnation and failure, and some may continue to seek new breakthroughs, at some point it becomes an eccentricity to adhere to an unsuccessful program.

The Expectations States Program illustrates both branching and competition. Status characteristic theory represents only one branch of the program. The idea of beliefs about one's own capacities or attributes operates as a central mechanism in theories about distributive justice, sources of self-evaluation, and personality characteristics. Core concepts such as expectation states, activation, and relevance play a role in each member of this family of theories. The theories use propositions based on these concepts to explain different phenomena: the conditions under which actors feel justly or unjustly rewarded, the process by which an actor arrives at a stable self-evaluation, and the way attribution of personality characteristics to others affects interpersonal relationships (Berger, Rosenholtz, and Zelditch, 1980). Expectation States researchers have designed confrontations with other programs such as, for example, equity theory (Webster and Smith, 1978) and sex-role socialization theory (Lockheed and Hall, 1976). Other researchers have confronted the Expectation States program with alternative theories based on power (Archibald, 1976) and behavioral demeanor (Lee and Ofshe, 1981).

One confrontation pitting status characteristic theory against self-concept theory occurred relatively early in the CRP. Since it serves to illustrate the process of choosing among competing theories, we will describe the case in some detail.

Self-concept theory (e.g., Rosenberg, 1979) offers an alternative explanation for many of the observation statements that are explained by status characteristic theory. Self-concept theory is not as explicitly formulated as status characteristic theory; for instance, it contains no scope conditions. The main argument, however, is clear. The self-concept is regarded as an enduring feature of a person's personality that operates in all situations to affect that person's behavior. A low self-concept is a generalized feeling of inferiority and incompetence, while a high self-concept is a generalized feeling of superiority and competence. The self-concept is formed during early experiences of the individual and is highly stable and resistant to change. People with low self-concepts have low opinions of their own worth, are likely to be nonparticipants in interaction, are deferential to others, and are highly susceptible to influence from others. People with high self-concepts are just the opposite. Proponents of this theory argue that, on the average, blacks and women have low self-concepts.

Clearly, there are some similarities between the two theories. But the differences are profound. Expectations based on states of a status characteristic are relative to the situation and the other people involved in the interaction. Self-concept is an attribute of the person and is not so dependent on the nature of the situation or on the other people with whom the person is interacting. Expectations based on status characteristics have to be activated in order to affect behavior in a given situation; self-concept is always activated and determinative of behavior. To oversimplify, status characteristic theory allows a person to be quiet in one situation and to be a leading participant in another; self-concept theory claims that quiet people will be low participants in all situations.

Which theory has greater explanatory power has not been settled definitively. The problem is to choose between an explanation based on properties of the individual (self-concept) and an explanation based on the properties of the situation (the individual's state of status characteristic relative to the other person or persons in the interaction). Some of the status characteristic research has addressed the question; and for those studies, status characteristic theory explains results which cannot be explained by self-concept theory. A few examples will illustrate how this process has proceeded.

In one type of status characteristic study, a subject interacts with a partner on a judgment task. The task to be successfully completed requires a fictional ability. One such task, called contrast sensitivity, involves a series of judgments, each of which requires a decision as to which of a pair of figures has more black areas. For each pair of figures, the subject makes an initial judgment, is told the judgment of his or her partner, and then makes a final judgment. The subject never actually sees the partner; all interaction takes place through a specially constructed machine that allows the subjects to express initial and final judgments by pressing buttons and to receive feedback about their partners' judgments by reading lights on their consoles. The feedback is controlled by the researcher and most of the time indicates to the subject that the partner disagrees with the initial judgment of the subject. The main indicator used in these studies is the number of times the subject changes initial judgments in the face of disagreement from the partner. Each treatment consists of putting many subjects through this situation, and treatments differ only with respect to status information given the subjects. In a two-treatment study, for example, the subjects in one treatment are told that their partner has a higher state of the status charactristic than they themselves possess; in the other treatment, they are told that they have a lower state than their partner. In one study, in which the subjects were all air force sergeants, air force rank was the status characteristic; those in one treatment were told their partner was an air force captain, while those in the second treatment were told their partner was an airman third class (the next-to-lowest rank in the Air Force). Since subjects never see their partners, and they exchanged information only by machine, the only information subjects had about their partners was what the researchers told them.

Suppose differences are observed between treatments in these studies; the air force study, for example, found that sergeants working with airmen third class were more resistant to changing their judgments than were sergeants working with captains (Berger et al., 1972). It is possible to explain those differences by assuming that the sergeants in one treatment have low self-concepts and those in the other treatments have high self-concepts. It is also possible to explain the differences using status characteristic theory. Before the study was done, however, the investigators recognized that they would have to control for the operation of self-concept in order to facilitate choice between the two competing theories. They planned their study to insure that the two groups of sergeants (those working with captains and those working with airmen third class) would be equivalent with respect to self-concept. In other words, for every sergeant with a high self-concept who worked with a captain, there would be a sergeant with a high self-concept who worked with an airman third class. Equating self-concept meant that if there were differences in resistance to influence, those differences could not be attributed to differential self-concepts, because the two groups were matched. Thus, observed differences could then be explained by status characteristic theory and not explained by self-concept theory. Many of the studies in this research program utilized a similar technique for controlling the operation of self-concept and thus produced a body of results that could be explained by one theory but not the other.

It should be clear, however, that the question of which theory has more explanatory power is still open, since there may be studies which can be explained by self-concept theory but not by status characteristic theory.

The use of fictional abilities in these studies is another important control facilitating the choice between self-concept theory and status characteristic theory. If these studies used a task involving, for example, mathematical ability, people's self-concepts about their own mathematical ability might be so strong that they would outweigh any status information. That is not really the central issue between the two theories, however; the central issue concerns the individual generalizing to new tasks. Self-concepts are supposed to generalize, although without scope conditions we do not know the limits of such generalizing. Status information generalizes to new tasks when the status characteristic is the only basis for forming expectations with respect to the ability that the new task requires. From the perspective of status characteristic theory, these fictional tasks are an essential control feature of the research design. With these fictional tasks—and several different ones have been used—status characteristic theory explains the results, whereas it is not clear when subjects generalize their self-concepts to new tasks and when they do not. More definitive choices between the two theories, however, must await the formulation of scope conditions for self-concept theory.

The importance of designing studies to provide the most informative comparisons is illustrated by the study involving race as a status characteristic, described earlier. When students are told about this study, the first question they ask is, "Why didn't the study compare a treatment where a black subject interacts with a white partner with the treatment where a white subject works with a black partner?" The answer is straightforward. If such a study had been conducted and black subjects had shown less resistance to influence than white subjects, the results could easily have been explained by asserting that blacks had lower self-concepts than whites. The study deliberately chose to compare white subjects interacting with a higher status white partner, and white subjects interacting with a black partner, controlling for the effects of self-concept in order to eliminate the self-concept explanation of differences that might be, and were, observed. One could follow up this study with one that compared black subjects interacting with black partners of lower status, with black subjects interacting with white partners.

Finally, studies have been conducted which have trained the low-status person to be especially competent at a task and have trained the high status person to recognize that competence (E. G. Cohen and Roper, 1972). These studies have shown that such expectation training generalizes to a new task and creates expectations based on states of the status characteristic. It is difficult to imagine such short-term training interfering with long-standing self-concepts. Such research, although it must still be viewed cautiously (since not every study has been successful in overcoming the effects of status), is of enormous practical significance. Improving the school performance of the low-status student might be accomplished by altering status conceptions rather than by attempting to alter enduring features of personality, such as self-concept. Furthermore, these studies suggest that the status conceptions of both high- and low-status people need to be modified; *any intervention program that operates only on low-status students is unlikely to succeed.* The emphasis in status characteristic theory—that expectations are relative to others involved in interaction—leads to treating both high- and low-status participants. The emphasis in self-concept theory—on the individual's self-concept—points to treating only those students with low self-concepts.

These examples illustrate how studies in a cumulative research program supplement one another; each study deals with some of the issues raised in prior studies and adds information by also considering issues that have not been raised previously. Having solidified the elimination of properties of the individual as explanations, later studies in the series would be less dependent on random assignment. Having demonstrated that the theory explains results from experiments using new tasks and fictional abilities, later studies could tackle tasks and abilities for which people had already formed expectations in order to determine how status information had interfered with these prior expectations. The process involves generalizing the theory, planning new empirical studies to evaluate the hypotheses derived from the generalized theory, and comparing alternative theories—the theory with external competitors or the original theory and its generalized version.

The discussion and analysis of the more advanced stages of a CRP contain within them a strategy for mature programs. Seeking new domains where some of the concepts and key assumptions of a CRP can generate new explanations represents one path to growth or, in the event of repeated failures, to the abandonment of the program. Sociologists have followed this path but usually before a mature program has developed, and this often results in the abandonment of the program. A research program built around a personality theory of the "authoritarian personality" exemplifies the problem; researchers employed the theory to explain everything from misperceptions of sexually oriented words to the emergence of totalitarian states so the ideas became increasingly vague, diminishing the content of the theory. Premature efforts to use a single principle to explain widely divergent phenomena usually does not promote growth but degrades the principle into a vague, all-encompassing statement that, in explaining everything, explains nothing.

A strategy that is more likely to advance a program is one that formulates new explanatory principles instead of stretching existing principles too thinly. Formulating new principles generates new problems and new solutions. When a CRP contains one or more well-developed theories, researchers can construct variants of the theory or theories. These use the core ideas of the CRP to create new knowledge claims and in this way theorists add to, rather than diminish, the content of the program.

The second element of the strategy for mature CRPs rests on the assumption that confrontation produces growth. When a mature program has established a firm theoretical and empirical foundation, researchers—both supporters and opponents of the CRP—should seek comparisons of the program's explanations with strong alternatives. If alternative theories exist, then the strategy involves designing a series of empirical studies that maximizes the possible comparisons among alternative explanations and thus facilitates choice. Each study in the series should supplement the comparisons provided by other studies and enhance the possibility that the end result will be a clear preference for one of the theories or, if not, then a new theory which encompasses both. If reasonable alternative theories do not exist, researchers in the program would do well to attempt to construct competitors to their own theories. While asking people to attack their own creations may seem to go against human psychology, it represents only a small extension of the thought experiments in which theorists like Albert Einstein conjectured a have indicated, range of competing ideas. After all, theories which survive strong attacks are more impressive than those which win out over weak competitors. Besides, who is better able to construct strong alternative theories than those researchers intimately familiar with the core elements of the program.

A SUMMARY AND TWO CONCLUSIONS

Chapters 15 and 16 have presented a conception of *cumulative research programs* based on viewing growth as an increase in the capacity for generating and solving theoretical and practical problems. We introduced the concept of explanatory power and developed a concept of generalization that did not depend on a logic of induction. The analysis suggested general questions for CRPs as well as questions directed to particular stages of development.

For early stages, criteria concern the stability of a phenomenon and the demonstration of some explanatory power for an idea. Moving to an intermediate stage requires formulating Simple Knowledge Structures leading eventually to a theory, generalizing the explanatory power of the original idea, testing it against relatively strong alternatives, developing explicit definitions, and improving research instruments. To continue to grow, mature programs in more advanced stages of development need to move from one well-supported theory to create a family of related theories sharing core ideas but dealing with different sets of phenomena. Continued growth also stems from confrontations with competing programs that address the same phenomena.

The discussion posed several suggestions for research strategies geared to the stage of development of a program and raised issues for a methodology of CRPs to address.

Our explication of CRPs points to two general conclusions, one proposing a resolution to the problem of criteria for the empirical evaluation of ideas and the second offering a central principle for the strategy of developing sociological knowledge.

By now the reader should be convinced that the question of the truth of universal knowledge claims and theories does not have a simple answer. While intersubjective testability demands that claims can be true or false, deciding on truth or falsity turns out to be very difficult indeed. We have stressed that empirical evaluation of ideas is a process but, even after many steps in that process, one does not have definitive answers. In practice, then, the requirement of testability means that there must be some conditions under which a sociologist will be willing to give up an idea or a theory. By redefining the problem in terms of research programs pursuing a core set of ideas, the formulation of this and the previous three chapters provides some provisional criteria and, although these criteria may be fuzzier than we are happy with, they do represent a direction for dealing with this very difficult problem.

Intellectual Property for Paralegals:
The Law of Trademarks, Copyrights, Patents, and Trade Secrets

(Second Edition)

Deborah E. Bouchoux, Esq.

THOMSON

DELMAR LEARNING

Australia Canada Mexico Singapore Spain United Kingdom United States

We propose that researchers should abandon a CRP in either of two circumstances:

1. **When an alternative program has demonstrated greater explanatory power over the key phenomena.**
2. **When a program can no longer generate new problem definitions and new problem solutions.**

The central strategic principle for developing knowledge emerges from the key role of explanation in a CRP. Growth entails expanding explanatory power. By seeking more powerful alternative explanations we promote growth, hence the principle is:

A science cannot accept anything as it is; it requires an explanation for everything.

Researchers often seek explanations for disconfirming results but rest content when observations support their hypotheses. At every stage of development, it is not sufficient to accept confirmation; one must look for possible alternative explanations for successful outcomes as well as for failures. Since no explanation is unique, even if there is a satisfactory explanation, the possibility always exists of finding a better one, that is, a more powerful one. The search itself promotes the growth of knowledge.

SUGGESTED READING

Stages of CRPs as they have been formulated in this book have not received attention in either the sociological or philosophical literature. The paper of Wagner and Berger cited above deals with the analysis of programs in relatively advanced stages of development. These authors present an analytic scheme for examining patterns of theoretical growth and apply it to two examples from the bargaining literature.

SEVENTEEN

Some
Final
Comments

Chapter 1 asserted that there was a better way to resolve conflicts about human social behavior than simply entitling everyone to his or her own opinion. The remaining chapters developed one better way. A better way is not an easier way: the path to sound sociological knowledge is long, difficult, and demanding. It requires individual and collective commitment as well as institutional and societal investments. Those who want guaranteed panaceas for society's problems, and want them now, are bound to be disappointed.

Some may say that a better way is not worth the effort. Society has neither the time to wait nor the resources to invest. After all, the human race, despite ignorance and prejudice, has survived up to now on hunch and hope. By trial and error, we have blundered through, and we can continue to do so.

This brings us back to value judgments and matters of faith. Even though we can point to successful sociological theories with practical applications—we have illustrated one such theory—it is always possible to claim that sociology does not deal with the really important problems of society and thus is not worth society's investment. The definition of "really important problems" ultimately depends on value judgments, as do all action decisions. No matter what problems may be solved with the aid of sociological theories, there will always be some critics who regard the contributions as trivial, the problems as unimportant, and the efforts misplaced. They will not be convinced, and we can only acknowledge the irreconcilable value conflict.

Some critics doubt that the strategy we have developed represents a better way. Actually, they question the objective of a rational, empirically based understanding of human social behavior. They worry that such an understanding will denigrate the wonderful mystery and uniqueness of human beings and relegate us to insignificant cogs in a machine-like universe. This position traces back to a nineteenth century view of science—a view held by many lay people and even some scientists—in which a thoroughgoing determinism applied to all action, human and nonhuman. Modern science rejects such determinism, and the approach developed in this book is consistent with individuality and historical uniqueness. To argue that some social action under some conditions can be explained by sociological theories is not to claim that all social behavior under all possible conditions is explainable. In fact, a major reason for our rejection of holism is that "wholes," whole persons or whole societies, are unique; they are not appropriate objects of general theory. Our insistence on the conditional nature of sociological knowledge is further recognition of the partial nature of scientific understanding.

It is a matter of faith that such partial understandings of human social behavior contained in sociological theories can be practically useful. Past successes or failures cannot prove or disprove the faith in the potential usefulness of a new theory; usefulness must be determined anew for every theory. When a sociologist begins to work on a problem, there is no guarantee that the work will lead to a theory with significant explanatory power or practical application. For a sociologist working on the development of theory, there is no alternative to such faith.

For lay supporters of sociological research, there is also no alternative to such faith. The fact that society regards a problem as important is neither a necessary nor sufficient condition for successful solution of that problem. The history of science is full of examples of research on significant problems that led nowhere and of research on apparently trivial problems that had enormous practical payoff. Society's attempt to tell sociologists what problems to investigate—through crash programs on alcoholism, crime, and poverty, to cite just a few examples—far too often has led to failure and frustration. Recognition that an element of faith is involved may avoid some of the failure and frustration. Such recognition does not require that society give sociology a blank check to study anything in any way.

Lay supporters of sociology, funders of research, and users of research results can best serve sociology and society by developing a sophistication that recognizes the possibilities and limitations of sociological research. While it is inappropriate to tell sociologists what problems to investigate, it is perfectly appropriate to ask the sociologists to justify their choices of problems. While it is inappropriate to tell sociologists how to study their problems, it is perfectly appropriate to require sociologists to explain and justify their strategies and to be sure that these justifications are acceptable to the relevant public. The consumer can ask questions that are sympathetic but also critical. A sociologist who wishes to apply knowledge can be asked about the adequacy of the knowledge base to be applied. A sociologist who wishes to advance the state of knowledge about a phenomenon can be asked about the availability of the conceptual tools necessary for such an advance. The issues raised throughout this book provide a number of questions which the sophisticated and sympathetic consumer can raise. Before summarizing these questions in a "Consumer's Guide to Sociological Research," we want to address some final comments to those who produce and those who apply sociological knowledge.

PRODUCING SOCIOLOGICAL KNOWLEDGE

The model for developing sociological knowledge that we have presented places heavy demands on the producers, whether they are doing basic or applied research. Many of us are drawn to research with an overly optimistic view of the perspiration to inspiration ratio. While moments of the excitement of discovery and the gratification of successful problem solving do occur, they occur as a result of perseverance, patience, and hard work. Commitments to long-term programs of research, perhaps, require a greater postponement of gratification than moving from topic to topic with each new study. The challenge of novelty and the excitement of being the first to explore new territory attract many of us and make it difficult to pursue the more mundane aspects of building cumulative knowledge. Kuhn's distinction between periods of "normal science" and scientific revolutions (Kuhn, 1970) is an appropriate metaphor: we all want to be revolutionaries rather than the plodders who carry out ordinary normal activities.

We can't all be revolutionaries. Furthermore, without an established structure of knowledge it is difficult to distinguish between a revolutionary advance and a "crackpot" illusion. As we have argued, only cumulative research programs will produce intersubjectively accepted structures of sociological knowledge. And while some CRPs may come about serendipitously, more are likely to result from intentional strategies.

We have proposed the search for explanations as a driving force in initiating and expanding CRPs. We have also argued that explanations we seek must be responsible and heuristic. Acceptable explanations are testable and generate consequences beyond the explananda that motivated them. We cautioned against the ubiquitous principle that purports to explain everything and, like the Delphic oracle, actually explains nothing.

If the search for explanations is the driving force of CRPs, the hallmarks of their success are the theories that are proposed, tested, and elaborated. While exploratory and descriptive studies as well as attempts to use sociological ideas to solve practical problems may contribute to the enterprise, comprehensive explanations require powerful theories that are rigorously stated and empirically supported. Theories as we have defined them do not serendipitously appear on the scene fully ripened. The theories develop over relatively long periods of time as a result of planned efforts of many researchers.

Intentional research strategies depend on analysis, and both the quality of the individual study and the likelihood of growth in the program increase with the quality of the analysis. The issues discussed throughout this book offer a series of analytic questions and provisional criteria for evaluating the answers to these questions.

A caution, however, is in order. Although we emphasize the critical importance of analysis and the necessity of an analytic approach, it is possible to have too much of a good thing. In this case, too much of good thing can be paralyzing.

While the principle in chapter 16 asserts that nothing is taken as is and that everything must be explained, we must qualify the application of the principle. Otherwise, we could find ourselves in the position of the parent who answers each "Why?" question of the child and receives another "Why?" in response. At some point, we must take an explanation as a given and not ask why or we fall into an infinite regress. In practice, infinite regress rarely traps producers of knowledge, but frequently inheres in some of the questions raised by critics of an investigation or theory.

It is also a "good thing" to question the assumptions underlying a study or a theory or a research strategy. We must recognize that we cannot question all assumptions all the time, however, and we must remember that no research is assumption free. Developing knowledge is a "bootstrap" operation; we pull ourselves up by making some assumptions which allow us to evaluate other ideas. An initial test of a knowledge claim may need to assume the reliability and validity of the indicators used, but, given support for the knowledge claim, we may use it in a subsequent study as a basis for evaluating the reliability and validity of the indicators. If we were unwilling to make the initial assumptions about the indicators, we would rule out any possibility of advancing our knowledge.

Cumulative research programs are critically important to any scientific discipline. While sociologists may generally agree with this point, they will disagree on the extent to which such programs exist in the field and on how interrelated the elements of a CRP must be. We can grant that there are a number of CRPs, but we must recognize that in many of them the elements are very loosely connected. Most of these CRPs are in early stages of development and some have shown relatively little growth over the years. Perhaps the loosely connected nature of some of these programs explains their lack of development. Perhaps some of the lack of advance stems from an inadequate additive conception of cumulation, rather than a conception that stress the program's ability to generate and solve new problems. Whether either of these explanations is true or not, we suggest that the delineation of explicit strategies, explicit questions, and explicit knowledge claims will serve to promote the growth of CRPs.

CRPs also provide benefits to the individual researcher. Researchers oriented to a program of research can avoid the impossible task of solving all problems in one study. They do not even have to know all the problems or recognize all the assumptions underlying their study. Such investigators understand that they will "get smarter" as the program progresses.

A second benefit accrues from the fact that CRP must be a collective enterprise. Researchers not only "get smarter" from their own work, but they gain from others doing closely related work even if the others advance alternative and competing explanations. While there has been much discussion of scientific communities, the ties in such communities depend on the degree of interrelatedness of the members' work. Scientists working on common problems in a CRP are most likely to form communities with close ties among members.

Another benefit of a CRP is that it allows, indeed requires, a plurality of methods. No research technique or metatheoretical orientation has a monopoly on the production of knowledge. At various stages of development, particular approaches or particular methods may be more appropriate than alternatives, but varied attacks on a sociological question can only enrich a program. Perhaps a greater recognition of this fact can serve to break down some of the artificial barriers that divide sociologists, barriers like the quantitative-qualitative controversy.

CRPs are not closed corporations. As long as sociological research is not classified "top secret," and not much sociology is, any producer can join and without an invitation. The producer need not be sympathetic to the program and even may want to reorient it. As soon as one attempts to build on, modify, criticize, or propose alternatives to the knowledge claims, or empirical findings, or other elements of the program, one has become a participant.

Since we consider CRPs essential to developing knowledge in the discipline and intellectually beneficial to the individual researcher, we believe that the trainers of sociological producers should devote considerably more attention to the problems, standards, requirements, and strategies of CRPs. We hope that this book has contributed to sensitizing producers to the critical place of CRPs. If we can get more producers to ask three key questions in a serious rather than a perfunctory way, we will have made a start. These questions are:

1. On what ideas, knowledge claims or findings from previous work can I build?
2. How will my proposed research advance the program by raising and/or solving new problems?
3. What next steps will follow from my research?

APPLYING SOCIOLOGICAL KNOWLEDGE

The first principle to reiterate is that applying knowledge inherently involves value judgments. Sociological knowledge, by itself, cannot determine what should be done to solve a problem. A body of theory, or a body of research results, may show the consequences of alternative actions; but those consequences must be evaluated on grounds that are outside the realm of knowledge—that is, on grounds of comparing alternative values. A theory could indicate that under certain conditions an affirmative-action program could enhance the morale of female workers in an organization, but the desirability of those consequences relative to other outcomes must still be weighed.

Our second principle is that available sociological knowledge, no matter how well developed, never exactly fits a practical situation. The application of knowledge always demands extrapolation from what is known. Theories with considerable explanatory power are still only partial explanations, dealing with only some aspects of the problem situation. Although a theory may predict affirmative-action consequences to female morale, unique feature of the organization, like an insensitive personnel manager, might upset the prediction. Factors outside the theoretical formulation will always operate, and judgment about the relative importance of these other factors will always be required.

In general, and this is our third principle, application always requires judgment and clinical insight in addition to theoretical knowledge. Application of knowledge is not mechanical process that can be accomplished by following a recipe. Practical situations, for example, usually violate the scope conditions of theory; only experience and artistic talent can allow the practitioner to decide whether the violations are serious enough to make the theory inapplicable. In applications, theoretical knowledge and clinical expertise are necessary complements to one another.

Complementarity cannot be overemphasized. A theory channels clinical insight and sensitizes the clinician to anticipate problems. In working with sex discrimination in an organization, for example, status characteristic theory sensitizes the clinician to the conditions under which sex would be a status characteristic, and to a concern with what other status characteristics might be operating. Only the clinician's expert historical knowledge of the organization can separate those organizational activities which are collective interdependent tasks from those which are individual functions. A knowledge base enhances the clinician's ability to deal with problems by providing tools for diagnosis and new alternative remedies; but the clinician's expertise makes the knowledge usable, by translating abstract ideas into concrete, situationally relevant actions.

When we speak of a knowledge base for solving practical problems, we mean the theoretical base, not a list of observation statements from empirical studies. An unconceptualized, and therefore unorganized, collection of empirical results does not provide an adequate set of guidelines for practical applications. As we have stressed repeatedly, we cannot generalize these empirical results to the new situation, for each inductive generalization is as likely to be wrong as right. We cannot simply assert that the results are applicable to the new situation, because the new situation is guaranteed to be different in many ways from the situation previously studied. We need guidelines to tell us when we can safely ignore those differences and when we must take them seriously. A theoretical base not only provides such guidelines, but also helps us to determine which empirical results are relevant to our practical problem and which are not. Hence, explicit, carefully formulated, empirically tested theory is a practical tool, not a pedantic luxury.

Solving practical problems, however, cannot await the full-blown development of theories. In the absence of well-established theories, can sociological ideas and sociological research aid in the solution of practical problems? The answer is ''Yes, but . . .'' In chapter 2, we noted that engineering takes the problem as given and uses whatever is available—knowledge, hunch, insight—in attempting to solve the problem. Certainly, sociological ideas and sociological studies can provide hunches and insights. But the status of hunches based on research is no more privileged than that of hunches derived from other sources, and the quality of the solution will depend on the quality of clinical judgment, not on the research that is used in making that judgment. Research can be suggestive, but it cannot justify any particular solution. The ultimate responsibility rests with the problem solver, and that responsibility cannot be abdicated by invoking the authority, "A study shows..." Too often, when clinical judgment and an empirical study are in conflict, we automatically reject clinical judgment although it is by no means clear that we should place our confidence in the empirical study. Solving practical problems demands ideas, judgment, and careful analysis of the problem situation and not mindless employment of the results of some empirical study. Research can aid in dealing with practical problems in another way, one that is familiar to practitioners. The fact-finding study, usually a survey, can provide useful information for diagnosing problems and designing remedies. But even fact-finding research is not self-justifying. A fact-finding study can provide the right answers to the wrong questions; it can generate irrelevant as well as relevant facts and further confuse rather than clarify the picture. Too often, fact-finding is undertaken as a substitute for thinking about the problem. When careful analysis of a problem indicates that information is needed and specifies the kinds of information required, fact-finding can be extremely useful. Research is then used in the service of rational judgment, not as a substitute for it.

This brings us to our final principle for applying knowledge. Theortical knowledge, no matter how well-established, and a body of empirical research, no matter how extensive, cannot guarantee successful problem solution. What we can guarantee is that the practitioner who employs well-established theory based on a body of empirical research is using the best available tools.

A CONSUMER'S GUIDE

One of the main objectives of this book is to present the reader, whether producer or consumer, with a different way to think about research. If we have stimulated consumers to think at all about research claims, we have accomplished part of our objective, since too many consumers simply take research claims at face value.

Thinking about research involves asking questions. Lay people, to be sophisticated consumers of sociological research, must adopt a critical analytical attitude. But a hypercritical stance is just as inappropriate as an uncritical one. Consumers can ask some questions and understand the answers, but there are some technical answers that consumers must be willing to take on faith. Even technical questions must be raised, however, so that consumers can serve as watchdogs to insure that the relevant public has done its job.

What kinds of questions can the consumer ask of sociological claims? This book has a few major themes that generate important questions for the consumer. Let us look at these and the questions they provide.

Scientific knowledge is theoretical knowledge collectively evaluated using reason and evidence. The first question a consumer can ask is, What is the theoretical basis of a research claim? This leads to a number of more specific questions: Does the claim come from a theory? How well established is the theory? How much research has addressed the theory? Is the theory part of a ongoing research program? Are there alternative theories which also explain the claim? Is the weight of available evidence clearly in support of one theory?

The logical relationship of the claim to a particular theory can also be questioned. How does the research claim fit into the theory? Is it a direct, deductive consequence of the theory, or an extrapolation from the theory? Is the claim within the scope of the theory? Asking these questions forces the consumer to ask whether the theory has explicit scope conditions and whether the scope statements can be generalized.

There are not many well-established sociological theories at the present stage of development of sociology, and the consumer cannot simply reject those claims which are not based on well-established theories. This brings us to a second major theme: *Research is a process.* Evaluating a research claim depends on the solution of too many problems (reliability, uniqueness, validity, and so on) to expect a single study to resolve them all. Only a few of the many assumptions underlying a claim can be evaluated in a single study. Finally, in explanatory research, one study can compare only a limited number of the important competing explanations.

Consumers, then, should be wary of claims based on single studies. The wariness translates into several questions directed at those claims advanced on the basis of a single study: Are there other studies that bear on the claim? What steps have been taken to insure that the observation statements are reliable? Is there any basis for ruling out the possibility that the empirical results are accidental or unique? (In other words, what reasons are there to believe that the results of the study are reproducible?) Have there been any efforts to test the instruments used to collect observations before they were employed in the study? What is the sociologist assuming about the phenomenon being investigated? In an opinion survey, for example, are the opinions assumed to be deeply held by the respondents, or only superficial? Are the techniques of data collection and analysis consistent with the investigator's assumptions about the phenomenon? As chapter 5 noted, it does not make much sense to analyze fine distinctions among superficially held opinions and, as chapter 9 pointed out, numerical scores may give a misleading impression of the precision of the observations.

Our third theme is: *Research claims must be explicit and communicable.* Even when examining a series of related studies, the consumer can inquire whether the relevant public agree on what the research claim means or whether the meaning is in dispute. It is always appropriate to ask, How explicit are the concepts used in the claim? How explicitly are the indicators tied to the concepts? In general, the consumer has every right to examine the relevance of observations to claims. Is relevance simply asserted? Is there some demonstration of relevance? What has been done to evaluate the validity of indicators and the truth of statements of initial conditions?

The fourth major theme is: *Scientific knowledge is conditional knowledge.* We have argued that conditions which define the circumstances of applicability of a sociological idea are not nitpicking qualifications but an essential part of scientific knowledge claims. It follows that the consumer should beware of unconstrained and unqualified claims. The consumer must ask, What are the guidelines for deciding when, where, and how to apply a research claim? In the absence of such guidelines, skepticism about "generalizations" of study results is clearly in order.

The theme that underlies all of the others is the concern that: *Research claims must be intersubjectively testable.* No research in any science is ever totally free from bias and subjective elements. The bias may come from a particular theoretical orientation, the value position of the researchers, or the limitations of humans as observers of phenomena. Acknowledging this fact of life, however, does not justify throwing up one's hands and concluding that everything is subjective. It is not an all-or-none proposition. It is erroneous to conclude that unless one is totally objective, one is subjective. The translation of literature from one language to another provides an appropriate analogy. It is impossible to translate exactly from one language to another because many words in one language do not have exact cognates in other languages; it is only possible to approximate the meanings intended in the original language. Despite wide recognition of this fact, no one has suggested that we abandon efforts to translate Proust or Tolstoy. Because we can only approximate objectivity, there is no reason to abandon efforts to be more and more objective by successive approximation.

Researchers must strive to be as objective as possible and consumers must promote such striving by asking telling questions: What has the researcher done to uncover sources of bias and correct for them? What has the community of researchers—the relevant public—done to examine critically a research claim in order to detect possible biases? The consumer can also scrutinize the relevant public. Has the community of researchers developed a strong, single orthodoxy that makes it incapable of detecting bias? Although the institutional norm of intersubjective testability provides some safeguards for dealing with biases, it still helps to have someone watch the watchman.

This consumer's guide should help create better watchers of the watchmen, more sophisticated consumers of sociological research. This, in turn, should have a beneficial effect on sociology itself. Higher standards for consumers should promote higher standards among the producers of sociological knowledge. This effect can occur only if consumers are sympathetic as well as critical, understanding the sociologist's objectives and the limits of science in general. Such understanding, combined with an appreciation of the efforts to transcend these limitations, can serve both sociology and society.

Sympathetic critics must recognize that sociologists are neither prophets nor magicians. We cannot guarantee truth. We cannot predict the future. We cannot deal with wholes—that is, with phenomena in all their complexity. Sociologists cannot solve all of the important problems of society. We may have nothing

THOMSON
™
DELMAR LEARNING

WEST LEGAL STUDIES

Intellectual Property for Paralegals:
The Law of Trademarks, Copyrights, Patents, and Trade Secrets, Second Edition
Deborah E. Bouchoux, Esq.

Career Education Strategic Business Unit:

Vice President:
Dawn Gerrain

Director of Editorial:
Sherry Gomoll

Developmental Editor:
Melissa Riveglia

Editorial Assistant:
Sarah Duncan

Director of Production:
Wendy A. Troeger

Production Manager:
Carolyn Miller

Production Editor:
Betty L. Dickson

Director of Marketing:
Wendy Mapstone

Cover Design:
Daniel Masucci

Library of Congress Cataloging-in-Publication Data

Bouchoux, Deborah E., 1950–
    Intellectual property for paralegals:
  the law of trademarks, copyrights,
  patents, and trade secrets /
  Deborah E. Bouchoux.— 2nd ed.
      p.   cm. — (West Legal Studies
  series)
    Includes index.
    ISBN-13: 978-1-4018-4287-1
    ISBN-10: 1-4018-4287-9
    1. Intellectual property—United
States.   2. Legal assistants—United
States—Handbooks, manuals,
etc.   I. Title.   I. Series.

KF2980.B678 2004
346.7304'8—dc22
                                            2003070119

NOTICE TO THE READER

useful to say about a problem that most concerns consumers at a particular moment in time. But, to paraphrase an eminent chemist who once addressed group of social scientists, the long-run obligation of sociologists to society is not to solve all society's pressing problems, but to bring to the understanding of social phenomena the same passion for truth and objectivity that has been so successful in the natural sciences.

REFERENCES

Allport, Gordon W.
1967   Attitudes. In *Readings in Attitude Theory and Measurement,* ed. Martin
            Fishbein. New York: Wiley.
Archibald, W. Peter
1976   Face-to-Face: The Alienating Effects of Class, Status and Power Divisions.
            American Sociological Review 41 (April): 819-37.
Berelson, Bernard, R., Paul F. Lazarsfeld, and William McPhee
1954   *Voting.* Chicago, Ill.: University of Chicago Press.
Berger, Joseph, Bernard P. Cohen, and Morris Zelditch, Jr.
1972   Status Conceptions and Social Interaction. *American Sociological Review*
            37 (June): 243-44.
Berger, Joseph, M. Hamit Fisek, Robert Z. Norman, and Morris Zelditch, Jr.
1977   *Status Characteristics and Social Interaction: An Expectation-States
            Approach.* New York: Elsevier.
Berger, Joseph, Susan J. Rosenholtz, and Morris Zelditch, Jr.
1980   Status Organizing Processes. *Annual Review of Sociology* 6: 241-55.
Blau, Judith R.
1974   Patterns of Communication among Theoretical High-Energy Physicists.
            Sociometry 37 (Sept.): 391-406.
Blau, Peter M.
1970   A Formal Theory of Differentiation in Organizations. *American Socio-
            logical Review* 35 (April): 201-18.
Brieger, Ronald
1976   Career Attributes and Network Structures: A Blockmodel Study of a
            Biomedical Research Specialty. *American Sociological Review* 41 (Feb.):
            117-35.
Bruner, Jerome S., and Cecily C. Goodman
1947   Value and Need as Organizing Factors in Perception. *Journal of Abnormal
            and Social Psychology* 42 (Jan.): 37-39.
Campbell, Donald T., and Julian C. Stanley
1963   Experimental and Quasi-Experimental Designs for Research on Teaching.
            In *Handbook of Research on Teaching,* ed. N. L. Gage. Chicago, Ill.: Rand
            McNally.
Chambliss, William J., and Robert B. Seidman
1971   *Law, Order, and Power.* Reading, Mass.: Addison-Wesley.
Chiricos, Theodore G., and Gordon P. Waldo
1975   Socioeconomic Status and Criminal Sentencing: An Empirical Assessment
            of a Conflict Proposition. *American Sociological Review* 40 (Dec.): 753-72.
1977   Reply to Greenberg, Hopkins and Reasons. *American Sociological Review*
            42 (April): 181-85.
Cohen, Bernard P., Joseph Berger, and Morris Zelditch, Jr.
1972   Status Conceptions and Interaction, A Case Study of the Problem of Develop-
            ing Cumulative Knowledge. In *Experimental Social Psychology,* ed. Charles
            G. McClintock. New York: Holt, Rinehart & Winston.

Cohen, Bernard P., Joan E. Kiker, and Ronald J. Kruse
1969   The Formation of Performance Expectations Based on Race and Education: A Replication. Technical Report no. 30. Stanford University: Laboratory for Social Research.

Cohen, Elizabeth G.
1976   Center for Interracial Cooperation. *Sociology of Education* 48 (Winter): 47-58.

Cohen, Elizabeth G., with Rachel Lotan and Lisa Catanzarite
1988   Can Expectations for Competence Be Treated in the Classroom? In *Status Generalization: New Theory and Research,* eds. Murray Webster and Martha Foschi. Stanford, Calif.: Stanford University Press.

Cohen, Elizabeth G., and Susan Roper.
1972   Modification of Inter-Racial Interaction Disability: An Application of Status Characteristic Theory. *American Sociological Review* 37 (Dec.): 643-55.

Cohen, Morris R., and Ernest Nagel
1934   *An Introduction to Logic and Scientific Method.* New York: Harcourt, Brace.

Collins, Barry E., and Harold Guetzkow
1964   *A Social Psychology of Group Processes for Decision-Making.* New York: Wiley.

Cook, Thomas D., and Donald T. Campbell
1979   *Quasi-Experimentation: Design and Analysis Issues for Field Settings.* Chicago, Ill.: Rand McNally.

Crane, Diana
1972   *Invisible Colleges: Diffusion of Knowledge in Scientific Communities.* Chicago, Ill.: University of Chicago Press.

Crews, Frederick
1987   In the Big House of Theory. *New York Review,* May 29, pp. 36-42.

Dalton, Melville
1959   *Men Who Manage.* New York: Wiley.

Davis, James A.
1959   A Formal Interpretation of the Theory of Relative Deprivation. *Sociometry* 22 (Dec.): 280-86.

Ehrlich, Paul R., and S. Shirley Feldman. The Race Bomb: Skin Color, Prejudice and
1978   Intelligence. New York: Ballantine Books.

Emerson, Richard
1962   Power-Dependence Relations. *American Sociological Review* 27 (Feb.): 21-32.

Entwisle, Doris R., and Murray Webster, Jr.
1974   Expectations in Mixed Racial Groups. *Sociology of Education* 47 (Summer): 301-18.

Freese, Lee
1980   The Problem of Cumulative Knowledge. In *Theoretical Methods in Sociology: Seven Essays,* ed. Lee Freese. Pittsburgh, Penn.: University of Pittsburgh Press.

Gibbs, Jack
1972   *Sociological Theory Construction.* Hinsdale, Ill.: Dryden Press.

Glass, Gene V., Barry McGaw, and Mary Lee Smith
1981   *Meta-analysis in Social Research.* Beverly Hills, Calif.: Sage.

Goldberg, Phillip
1968   Are Women Prejudiced Against Women? *Trans-Action* 5 (April): 28-30.

Guttman, Louis
1944   A Basis for Scaling Qualitative Data. *American Sociological Review* 9 (April): 139-50.
Halfpenny, Peter
1982   *Positivism and Sociology: Explaining Social Life.* London: George Allen & Unwin.
Harris, Marvin
1978   *Cows, Pigs, Wars and Witches—The Riddles of Culture.* New York: Vintage Books.
Hempel, Carl G.
1965   A logical Appriasal of Operationism. In *Aspects of Scientific Explanation.* New York: Free Press.
Hollander, E. P.
1958   Conformity, Status and Idiosyncrasy Credit. *Psychological Review* 65 (March): 125.
Homans, George C.
1950   *The Human Group.* New York: Harcourt Brace, Jovanovich.
1964   Contemporary Theory in Sociology. In *Handbook of Modern Sociology,* ed. Robert E. L. Faris. New York: Rand McNally.
Hopkins, Anthony
1977   Is There a Class Bias in Criminal Sentencing? *American Sociological Review* 42 (April): 176-77.
Hyman, Herbert H., W. J. Cobb, J. J. Feldman, C. W. Hart, and C. H. Stember
1954   *Interviewing in Social Research.* Chicago, Ill.: University of Chicago Press.
Katzer, Jeffrey, Kenneth H. Cook, and Wayne W. Crouch
1978   *Evaluating Information.* Reading, Mass.: Addison-Wesley.
Kemeny, John G., J. L. Laurie Snell, and Gerald L. Thompson
1966   *Introduction to Finite Mathematics.* 2d ed. Englewood Cliffs, N.J.: Prentice-Hall.
Kuhn, Thomas S.
1970   *The Structure of Scientific Revolutions,* rev. ed. Chicago, Ill.: University of Chicago Press.
Lakatos, Imre
1970   Falsification and the Methodology of Scientific Research Programs. In *Criticism and the Growth of Knowledge,* eds. Imre Lakatos and Alan Musgrave. Cambridge: Cambridge University Press.
La Piere, Richard T.
1934   Attitudes versus Actions. *Social Forces* 13 (Dec.): 230-37.
Lee, Margaret, and Richard Ofshe
1981   The Impact of Behavioral Style and Status Characteristics on Social Influence: A Test of Two Competing Theories. *Social Psychology Quarterly* 44 (June): 73-82.
Lenski, Gerhard
1966   *Power and Privilege.* New York: McGraw-Hill.
Lieberson, Stanley
1985   *Making It Count: The Improvement of Social Research and Theory.* Berkeley: University of California Press.
Light, Richard J., and David B. Pillemer
1984   *Summing Up: The Science of Reviewing Research.* Cambridge, Mass.: Harvard University Press.

Likert, Rensis
1932   A Technique for the Measurement of Attitudes. *Archives of Psychology* 140 (June): 1-55.
Lockheed, Marlaine E., and Kay P. Hall
1976   Conceptualizing Sex as a Status Characteristic: Applications to Leadership Training Strategies. *Journal of Social Issues* 32 (Summer): 111-24.
McGuire, William J.
1985   The Nature of Attitudes and Attitude Change. In *The Handbook of Social Psychology*, 3d ed., eds. Gardner Lindzey and Elliot Aronson. New York: Random House.
Martin, Michael W., and Jane Sell
1985   The Effect of Equating Status Characteristics on the Generalization Process. *Social Psychology Quarterly* 48 (June): 178-82.
Masterman, Margaret
1970   The Nature of a Paradigm. In *Criticism and the Growth of Knowledge*, eds. Imre Lakatos and Alan Musgrave. Cambridge: Cambridge University Press.
Merton, Robert K.
1949a   The Bearing of Sociological Theory on Empirical Research. In *Social Theory and Social Structure*. Glencoe, Ill.: Free Press.
1949b   The Bearing of Empirical Research on Sociological Theory. In *Social Theory and Social Structure*. Glencoe, Ill.: Free Press.
1973   *The Sociology of Science*, ed. Norman W. Storer. Chicago, Ill.: University of Chicago Press.
Nagel, Ernest
1961   *The Structure of Science*. New York: Harcourt Brace Jovanovich.
Park, Robert E.
1928   The Bases of Race Prejudice. *The Annals* 140 (Nov.): 11-20.
Pfeffer, Jeffrey, and Gerald R. Salancik
1978   *The External Control of Organizations*. New York: Harper and Row.
Phillips, D.C.
1976   *Holistic Thought in Social Science*. Stanford, Calif.: Stanford University Press.
Popper, Karl R.
1959   *The Logic of Scientific Discovery*. New York: Basic Books.
Reich, Charles
1970   *The Greening of America*. New York: Random House.
Rosenberg, Morris
1979   *Conceiving the Self*. New York: Basic Books.
Rowan, Brian, Steven T. Bossert, and David C. Dwyer
1983   Research on Effective Schools: A Cautionary Note. *Educational Researcher* 12 (April): 24-31.
Schuman, Howard, and Stanley Presser
1981   *Questions and Answers in Attitude Surveys: Experiments on Question Form, Wording and Context*. New York: Academic Press.
Seashore, Marjorie J.
1968   The Formation of Performance Expectations for Self and Other in an Incongruent Status Situation. Unpublished Ph.D. dissertation, Department of Sociology, Stanford University.
Spaeth, Joe L.
1985   Job Power and Earnings. *American Sociological Review* 50 (Oct.): 603-17.
Spencer, Meta
1976   *Foundations of Modern Sociology*. Englewood, Cliffs, N.J.: Prentice-Hall.

Stouffer, Samuel A.
1950   Some Observations on Study Design. *American Journal of Sociology* 40
            (Jan.): 355-61.
Stouffer, Samuel A., Edward A. Suchman, Leland C. Devinney, Shirley A. Star, and Robin
M. Williams, Jr.
1949   *The American Soldier: Studies in Social Psychology in World War II.*
            Vol. I: Adjustment during Army Life. Princeton, N.J.: Princeton University
            Press.
Torrance, E. P.
1955   Consequences of Power Differences on Decision-Making in Permanent and
            Temporary Three-Man Groups. In *Small Groups,* eds. A. Paul Hare, Edgar
            F. Borgatta, and Robert F. Bales. New York: Knopf.
Treiman, Donald J., and Kermit Terrell
1975   Sex and the Process of Status Attainment: A Comparison of Working Women
            and Men. *American Sociological Review* 40 (April): 174-200.
Underwood, Benton J.
1957   *Psychological Research.* Englewood Cliffs, N.J.: Prentice-Hall.
Villemez, Wayne J.
1977   Occupational Prestige and the Normative Hierarchy: A Reconsideration.
            Pacific Sociological Review 20, no. 3 (July): 455-72.
Wagner, David G., and Joseph Berger
1985   Do Sociological Theories Grow? *American Journal of Sociology* 90 (Jan.):
            697-729.
Walton, John
1966   Discipline, Method and Community Power: A Note on the Sociology of
            Knowledge. *American Sociological Review* 31 (Oct.): 684-89.
Webster, Murray A., Jr.
1977   Equating Characteristics and Social Interaction: Two Experiments. *Socio-*
            metry 40 (March): 41-50.
Webster, Murray A., Jr., and Martha Foschi, eds.
1988   *Status Generalization: New Theory and Research.* Stanford, Calif. Stanford
            University Press.
Webster, Murray A., Jr., and Leroy Smith
1979   Justice and Revolutionary Coalitions: A Test of Two Theories. *American*
            Journal of Sociology 84 (Sept.): 267-92.
Wolff, Kurt H., ed.
1950   *The Sociology of Georg Simmel.* Glencoe, Ill.: Free Press.

INDEX

Abstract, definition of, 76
Abstractions, shared, 131
Action, 58
  consistent, 142, 143
  decisions, 30, 32
  relationship to knowledge, 27-28, 30, 33
Activation, 211-13, 219
Additivity, 168
Advocacy social science, 47
Affirming the consequent, 252
Allport, Gordon W., 140, 141, 142
Alternative explanations, 263-64, 266-68, 271, 272, 274, 285-86, 288, 314
  constructing the set of, 268-73
  limited set, 261
  principles for choosing among, 258-59, 270
Analysis, 10, 24
  definition of, 24
  framework for, 87
  of theory, 218-24
Antecedent conditions, 84, 229-30
Anti-Positivists, 43-44
Applied science, 52, 55, 56, 57, 58-59
Arbitrariness, 130-31
Archibald, W. Peter, 320
Artifactual problems, 279
  selection bias, 279
  interviewer bias, 279
Artifactual relationship. *See* Relationship, as artifact
Assertions, 71, 184
  content of, 221
Assignment, 212
Assumptions, 183, 184-85, 188, 190, 196, 218, 220-21
  example of, 186
Attitude, 140-41, 143
  connotative definition of, 140, 142
Axioms, 184

Bacon, Francis, 69
Basic science, 52, 53, 54, 58-59, 60, 65
  activity of, 54
  distinct features of, 53

principal concern of, 54
  problems of, 54
Basic science and applied science
  continuity between, 55-56
  engineering distinguished from, 56
Basic science, applied science and engineering
  distinct orientations of, 53, 57
  distinction among, 53
Before-after control group design, 276
Behavior, kinds of, 216
Berelson, Bernard R., 119, 180
Berger, Joseph, 200, 205, 219, 223, 294, 299, 317, 319, 320
Bernoulli, Daniel, 55
Bernoulli's Principle, 55
Bias(es)
  anti-computer, 283
  interviewer, 279-80, 282
  question, 280
  selection, 279, 280-82
  systematic, 97
  upward, 98
  value, 34, 41
Blau, Judith R., 292
Blau, Peter M., 186-87, 188, 190
Bossert, Steven T., 286
Brieger, Ronald, 292
Bruner, Jerome S., 39

CRP. *See* Cumulative research program(s)
Campbell, Donald T., 251, 253, 255
Calculus of propositions, 227, 228-30
  using, 230-38
Cardinal numbers, 168, 169, 172
Cells
  definition of, 103-4
  examples of, 104-11
Center for Interracial Cooperation, 218
Chambliss, William J., 165-66, 287
Chiricos, Theodore G., 165-66, 287
Cobb, W.J., 280
Cohen, Bernard P., 200, 205, 219, 316-18, 322
Cohen, Elizabeth G., 218, 306, 318, 323

In memory of my mother
Mabel Kenney Eckmann